Table of Contents

Introduction

Since the tragic division of the Korean Peninsula, South Korea has been continually the main target of North Korea's diverse threats. [1] The seriousness of the North Korean threat became apparent with the sinking of the South Korean naval vessel *Cheonan* and the artillery attack on Yeonpyong Island in 2010. There remains a high possibility of additional North Korean military provocations designed to relieve internal problems related to a power struggle.

After the death of Kim Jong-il, the political situation in North Korea became increasingly unstable as power transferred to Kim Jong-un. There has been a growing concern about the chaotic aftermath of a regime collapse in the North. General James D. Thurman, the commander of U.S. Forces in Korea, stated in his Senate Armed Services Committee confirmation hearing that South Korea and the United States should prepare to cope with the complexity of North Korea's possible regime collapse. [2] Under these circumstances, South Korea needs to look ahead to the problems it may face and prepare to counter any North Korean insurgency that might result from the expansion of conflicts between political power groups. [3] A collapse in the North has a high possibility of triggering massive civilian defections to South Korea or China, which could lead to the mass murder of civilians by a new power group attempting to control the Northern population. As a result, there would be an increased likelihood of a humanitarian crisis and social disorder due to the emergence of multiple armed groups. The mass confusion in North Korea also

[1] The term South Korea refers to the Republic of South Korea in this study. In all places where the word North Korea is used it means the Democratic People's Republic of Korea.

[2] General Thurman stressed that "the U.S.-South Korea Combined Forces Command must continue readiness preparations to fight and win a war with North Korea and at the same time prepare to deal with the complexity of a regime collapse and the attendant consequences." In The Korea Times, "General Thurman urges preparation for North Korea regime collapse," (20 June, 2011). http://www.koreatimes.co kr /www/news/nation/ 2011/06/113_89816 html (accessed 21 July, 2011).

[3] Insurgency is defined as "an organized, protracted politico-military struggle designed to weaken the control and legitimacy of an established government, occupying power, or other political authority while increasing insurgent control." In U.S. Army Field Manual 3-24: *Counterinsurgency* (Washington, DC: U.S. Department of the Army, 2006), 1-1.

would deteriorate the security situation within and beyond the Korean Peninsula. Thus, South Korea needs to consider humanitarian intervention to protect civilians from the violation of human rights and to prevent the expansion of insecurity in the region due to WMDs in particular. The South's intervention would presumably trigger a Northern insurgency led with armed groups resisting reunification by the South.

North Korea is a hybrid threat with nuclear weapons, approximately 200,000 Special Forces, and a large number of conventional forces.[4] The threat this poses to South Korea in the event of the rogue regime's collapse would be extremely complex and dangerous. Moreover, the interaction of North Korea's political, social, and economic spheres would unpredictably increase the complexity in the operational environment and make more difficult the identification of solutions to the nation's problems. In this regard, South Korea first needs to grasp T.E. Lawrence's aphorism that "Making war upon insurgents is messy and slow, like eating soup with a knife."[5] That is, there needs to be an understanding of how major operations and counterinsurgency (COIN) differ in nature.[6] One concern is that superior conventional capability does not necessarily guarantee superiority in COIN operations.[7]

Within this context, South Korea still lacks a sufficient operational approach to conducting a COIN campaign despite its increased conventional capability and counter-guerrilla

---

[4] See the definition of a hybrid threat in U.S. Army Doctrine Publication 3-0, *Unified Land Operations* (Washington, DC: Headquarters, Department of the Army, 2011), 4. "A Hybrid threat is the diverse and dynamic combination of regular forces, irregular forces, terrorist forces, criminal elements, or a combination of these forces and elements all unified to achieve mutually benefitting effects."

[5] John A. Nagl,. *Learning to Eat Soup With a Knife: Counterinsurgency Lessons from Malaya and Vietnam* (Chicago: University of Chicago Press, 2002), xii.

[6] Counterinsurgency consists of "military, paramilitary, political, economic, psychological and civic actions taken by a government to defeat an insurgency." FM 3-24, *Counterinsurgency*, (Washington, D.C.: Department of the Army, 2006), 1-1.

[7] Jeffrey Record, *Beating Goliath: Why Insurgencies Win* (Washington D.C.: Potomac Books, 2009), Viii.

and counter-terrorism experience.[8] Accordingly, the findings of this study include recommendations for improving South Korea's COIN operations. Meeting the requirements for COIN could potentially establish conditions for better stability on the Korean Peninsula and avoid the mistakes South Koreans made before the Korean War. History shows that the South was not prepared to counter the invasion by North Korea even though indications of turmoil on the Peninsula were revealed through the spread of insurgency sparked in the Jeju islands.

The foundation of this monograph is the premise that a regime collapse in the North is likely, and that the South will be involved in COIN operations on the Peninsula. Moreover, there currently appear to be operational shortfalls in the knowledge, planning, and potential execution of COIN within the South Korean military. This monograph raises one primary and three secondary questions. The primary research question: "How can the South Korean military improve its capacity to conduct counterinsurgency in a complex environment?" Answering this primary research question determines how the South Korean army can effectively address insurgents armed with hybrid threats from the North. To do so, this study uses the U.S. Department of Defense's capabilities organization construct referred to as DOTMLPF, consisting of doctrine, organization, training, material, leadership and education, personnel, and facilities. DOTMLPF, as a problem-solving construct, provides a tool to collect all of the potential solutions for each of the gaps identified by assessing current capabilities and desired capabilities.[9]

---

[8] The definition of irregular warfare, guerrilla tactics, and terrorism tactics helps to clarify the relations between the terms and insurgency. "Irregular warfare is a violent struggle among state and non state actors for legitimacy and influence over a population. This broad form of conflict has insurgency, counterinsurgency, and unconventional warfare as the principal activities." FM 3-0, *Operations* (Washington, DC: Headquarters, Department of the Army, 2008), 2-10. Guerrilla tactics feature "hit-and-run attacks by lightly armed groups. Insurgents using guerrilla tactics usually avoid decisive confrontations unless they know they can win." Terrorist tactics employ "violence primarily against noncombatants. It can be effective for generating popular support and altering the behavior of governments." Guerrilla and terrorist tactics are tactics of insurgency. FM 3-24, 3-18.

[9] U.S. Army Training Doctrine Command (TRADOC), *Capabilities-Based Assessment (CBA) Guide Version 3.1* (Washington, D.C.: Department of the Army, 2010), D-7.

3

This monograph examines solutions for the South Korean military within three of these commodity areas: doctrine, organization, and leadership and education. Moreover, it applies the Capability-Based-Assessment (CBA) process model to answer the above three questions. [10] "The CBA is the analytic basis of the Joint Capabilities Integration and Development System (JCIDS) used by the U.S. Department of Defense. It includes a three-phased process: Functional Area Analysis (FAA), Functional Needs Analysis (FNA), and Functional Solutions Analysis (FSA). These phases identify conditions-based capability requirements, capability shortfalls when comparing existing capabilities to requirements, and non-material or material approaches to address those gaps, respectively." [11]

There are three secondary research questions that aim to determine areas where South Korea's counterinsurgency might be improved.

- Question 1: "What capabilities must the South Korean Army possess in order to accomplish required missions in case of a regime collapse in the North?"
- Question 2: "Which of the required capabilities does the South lack for coping with the complex insurgent challenges?"
- Question 3: "What Doctrine, Organization, and Leadership and Education solution approaches of DOTMLPF may the South's Army implement in order to mitigate the gaps?" [12]

Outputs from the process of FAA, FNA, and FSA respectively meet the requirements of research questions 1, 2, 3. Answering Question 1 requires knowledge of the operational environment and the character of the North's potential insurgency. Defining the character of a North Korean insurgency campaign is essential in order to recognize the conditions under which

---

[10] Ibid., 5. Below FAA, FNA, and FSA come from the same source.

[11] Ibid., 4. This is originally quoted from *Manual for the Operations of the Joint Capabilities Integration and Development System: JCIDS Manual* (Washington, D.C.: Department of the Army, 2009), A-1.

[12] U.S. Training Doctrine Command (TRADOC) Guide, *Capabilities-Based Assessment (CBA) Guide Version 3.1* (Washington, D.C.: Department of the Army, 2010), A-5. Research questions use sample contents to the essential elements of analysis (EEA) level for a generic Capability-Based Assessment (CBA).

the South Korean Army will conduct COIN operations. Once the character of the insurgency is defined, then the lists of missions and capabilities for dealing with this operational environment, as well as the conditions and standards for success for the South's counterinsurgency efforts, will become apparent. Answering Question 2 will identify the capabilities the South Korean Army currently possesses or lacks. It is especially helpful for identifying capability gaps. Question 3 provides Doctrine, Organization, and Leadership and Education solutions that will help to mitigate the gaps in South Korea's future COIN operations. Doctrinal viewpoints seek to forge the concept and methodology of operational art and design in terms of "Learn and Adapt." Organizational views pursue unity of efforts among the armed services and other agencies through a comprehensive South Korean interagency COIN operation. Finally, the leadership aspect focuses on the application of mission command from a perspective of outmaneuvering the insurgency within a required period.

Examining theory and practice in the study of COIN helps to support any recommendation of requirements for South Korea's COIN operations. The comparison method and approach allows a determination of whether South Korea's current COIN efforts are sufficient. A qualitative approach will be chosen to describe lessons learned from contemporary COIN operations and an interpretation of the data obtained through various materials. Sources of materials were the Combined Arms Research Library, School of the Advanced Military Studies (SAMS) text books, and U.S. Army Field Manuals, as well as U.S. websites for the Department of Defense, the Department of State, and other agencies. A quantitative research approach will also be utilized to gain and analyze the maximum amount of information from past COIN cases. The monograph argues that the operational environment on the Korean Peninsula may demand a campaign to counter a North Korean insurgency armed with hybrid threats and that COIN and operational art provide the best approach to managing such a conflict. Thus, this monograph analyzes the strategic context that South Korea may face and seeks to identify required capabilities, distill imperatives for Korea's COIN environment, and determine the requirements for Korea's COIN operations.

Theoretical Foundations: COIN and Operational Art

Knowledge of the theoretical and doctrinal foundations would be beneficial for analyzing the requirements of South Korea's COIN operations. COIN theory describes operational environment, insurgency, and the focal principles of COIN operations. Although there is no one-size-fits-all approach to COIN operations, a theory taken from one COIN campaign can be applied to another campaign. The South's own history with counterinsurgencies demonstrates the immutable nature of insurgency that transcends time and space. Operational art then includes the origin and evolution of operational art and its application to COIN.

Counterinsurgency

The nature of COIN, according to the *US Government Counterinsurgency Guide*, is dependent on the complex interaction of three key factors: "the characteristics of the environment in which it takes place; the nature of the insurgent group; and the nature of the counterinsurgent forces."[13] Within this context, it is worthwhile to explore the operational environment and then continue with a discussion of the insurgency and COIN theory.

Operational Environment

Operational environments, as defined in FM 3-0, are "a composite of the conditions, circumstances, and influences that affect the employment of capabilities and bear on the decisions of the commander."[14] The increasingly complex nature of the COIN environment makes it

---

[13] Bureau of Political-Military Affairs, Department of State, *U.S. Government Counterinsurgency Guide* (Washington, D.C.: Department of State.2009), 12.

[14] FM 3-0, *Operations* (Washington, D.C.: Department of the Army, 2008), 1-1.

difficult for counterinsurgents to cope with insurgent threats due to the interaction of a complex array of factors. FM 3-24 *Counterinsurgency* describes eight influences on current operational environments: Population Explosion; Urbanization; Globalization; Technology; Religious Fundamentalism; Resource Demand; Climate Change and Natural Disasters; Proliferation of Weapons of Mass Destruction and Effects.[15]

Although the operational environment influences the conduct of warfare regardless of the type of conflict, the extent to which operational environment influences motivation and actions is the difference between regular and irregular warfare. Unlike conventional military warfare, COIN has no distinctive front lines that can help assess progress. Further, human environmental factors such as political, economic, and social conditions are no less important than military factors in deciding the outcome of insurgent warfare. Thus there is a need to understand both the physical and the human dimensions of the environment in COIN operations. Bard E. O'Neill, in *Insurgency & Terrorism*, states that "a careful examination of the physical and human dimensions of the environment is a good starting point for analyzing an insurgency."[16] An assessment of physical aspects, such as the terrain, climate, and transportation-communication system, provides insight into the strategy and forms of violence characterizing the insurgency. For example, large areas with heavy jungle or mountains and poor roads, as in the Philippines, Vietnam, and Afghanistan aid guerrilla operations despite technological development in detection and air mobility.[17] On the other hand, human aspects of the environment are decisively influential to success or failure in COIN operations because of the importance of non-military factors in irregular forms of warfare. Therefore COIN requires a solid understanding of the relevant social,

---

[15] FM 3-24, 1-2.

[16] Bard E. O'Neill, *Insurgency and Terrorism: From Revolution to Apocalypse* (Dulles VA: Potomac Book, 2005), 88.

[17] Ibid.

cultural, economic, political, and security conditions as well as a knowledge of insurgent motivations, goals, and methods.

Nature of Insurgency

Insurgency is a subset of warfare included in the category of irregular warfare. Its long history is as old as other types of warfare. Although new types of insurgent strategy and tactics emerged with technological developments and globalization, many common characteristics from ancient times remain. FM-3-24 *Counterinsurgency,* reflecting the definitions of many COIN theorists, defines insurgency as "an organized, protracted politico-military struggle designed to weaken the control and legitimacy of an established government, occupying power, or other political authority while increasing insurgent control."[18] This definition stresses the protracted nature, the comprehensive political and military approaches, and the purpose of insurgency. Bard E. O'Neill describes insurgency as "a struggle between a non-ruling group and the ruling authorities in which the non-ruling group consciously uses political resources and violence to destroy, reformulate, or sustain the basis of legitimacy of one or more aspects of politics."[19] His definition delineates the cause of insurgency to be closely related to politics. Insurgents seek to overthrow the government or to form an autonomous entity through a combination of force, propaganda, subversion, and political mobilization. This monograph uses the definition described in FM 3-24 *Counterinsurgency.*

Insurgent motives are the basis for the different types of insurgencies as described by FM 3-24, *Counterinsurgency.* The manual presents six types of insurgencies related to insurgent motives. This archetype framework can aid counterinsurgents in thinking about the overall challenges in dealing with insurgencies. These challenges include: root causes of the insurgency;

---

[18] FM 3-24, 1-1.

[19] Ibid., 15.

the extent to which the insurgency enjoys internal and external support; the basis on which the insurgents appeal to the target population; the insurgents' motivation and depth of commitment; likely insurgent weapons and tactics; and the operational environment in which insurgents seek to initiate and develop their campaign and strategy.[20] Each insurgency has its own characteristics, and all insurgents use different means and ways to achieve their ultimate goals. Due to their weak capability, insurgents do not utilize a direct, conventional approach in confronting government forces. Instead, they pursue indirect approaches such as hit-and-run tactics to exhaust the strength of the counterinsurgents. With regard to insurgent forms of warfare, guerrilla warfare and terrorist attacks are the most common forms of offensive action. The purposes, targets, activities, and scale of organization determine insurgency tactics. Likewise, operational environment, goals, and motivations determine insurgent strategies.

There are six broad insurgent strategies: conspiratorial, military-focus, urban-warfare strategy, protracted popular war, identity-focused, and composite approaches.[21] A conspiratorial approach is the strategy of insurgents when a few insurgent leaders aim to seize power and provoke a revolution quickly. The Bolshevik Revolution in 1907 is a case in point. Military-focused approaches, like the focoist approach, rely highly on military force to create the conditions needed to seize control of government. Insurgents may apply conventional warfare, depending on their ends, ways, and means. Urban terrorism is an approach employed by small insurgent groups who do not need much popular support. As societies are urbanized, the strategy becomes successful and effective. Iraqi extremists applied this approach. The Maoist 'Protracted Warfare' model was a significant type of insurgency for the 20th Century with clearly defined

---

[20] Ibid., 1-5.

[21] Bard E. O'Neill, 45-67. The description below the six related insurgent strategies refers to the same source.

objectives and a sequenced approach to achieve them.[22] Mao's approach comprises three phases: strategic defensive, strategic stalemate, and strategic counteroffensive. The protracted strategy incorporates economic sabotage and terrorism into the strategic approach. The approach is complex to cope with because it uses guerrilla tactics and terrorism simultaneously in different places aiming at multiple politico-military logical lines of operations (LLOs). An identity-focused approach needs support from people with a common identity, such as an ethnic group, a religious group, or people with a particular ideological affiliation. The strategy is becoming common in contemporary insurgency and is often combined with a military-focused approach. Finally, composite approaches seek to adapt more than one strategy to fit into given circumstances. Within a single operational area, many insurgent entities may exist. Moreover, multiple actors may increase the complexity of COIN operations. Modern insurgencies are linked by dynamic networks and are increasingly turning to complex and unpredictable uses of violence with widely diverse goals.[23] An insurgent approach, as described above, differs from the others depending on its goal and condition. However, all insurgents need a common basic requirement for success: the support of the civilian population. Therefore, insurgents take strategic initiatives at the early stage and seek to evolve through a series of stages supported by the disaffected population.

Nature of Counterinsurgency Effort

FM 3-24 *Counterinsurgency* defines COIN as "military, paramilitary, political, economic, psychological and civic actions taken by a government to defeat an insurgency."[24] COIN is a complex set of warfare activities requiring comprehensive civilian and military efforts. There exists a basic difference between COIN and conventional warfare. COIN puts a premium on

---

[22] Ibid.

[23] Ibid.

[24] FM 3-24, 1-1.

gaining popular support, while conventional warfare emphasizes destruction of the enemy. Bard O'Neill postulates that COIN success depends on its integration with political, judicial, administrative, diplomatic, economic and social policies because COIN is a larger political-military struggle.[25] FM 3-24 describes eight historical principles for COIN:[26]

- Legitimacy is the main objective.
- Unity of effort is essential.
- Political factors are primary.
- Planners must understand the environment.
- Intelligence drives operations.
- Insurgents must be isolated from their cause and support.
- Security under the rule of law is essential.
- Counterinsurgents should prepare for a long-term commitment.

With regard to legitimacy, counterinsurgents can achieve effective governance through the combined use of military and nonmilitary means. A government may destroy the insurgent forces by overwhelming tangible means, but destruction does not necessarily translate into success in COIN. The insurgent seeks to take advantage of the root causes of the insurgency and acquire personnel, supplies, and information from the public. Thus the primary imperative for restoring legitimacy is to address the grievances that may have fueled support for the insurgency in terms of social, economic, and political discontent at the grassroots. The 2011 Arab Spring revolutions in North Africa and the Middle East demonstrate that governments that failed to address growing grievances of their people paid or may soon pay the price for their neglect. Unity of effort is essential to COIN operations and requires all elements of national power. Efforts to redress political problems are essential to achieving the desired end state in COIN, given that insurgency is mostly designed to seize political power. COIN may begin with military action to protect the population by destroying insurgents, but then political factors are addressed to

---

[25] Bard E. O'Neill, 164.

[26] FM 3-24, 1-20-24.

strengthen legitimate governance. Consequently, COIN needs to put a premium on political factors to achieve the end state.[27]

The remaining five of the eight historical principles are related to environment, intelligence, and public support. As stated previously under operational environment, an effective COIN operation needs a heavy emphasis on knowledge of the environment where counterinsurgents conduct operations. Based on an understanding of the COIN environment, counterinsurgents seek to acquire intelligence to verify whether they are moving in the right direction. Intelligence plays a primary role in eliminating the root causes of insurgency. Moreover, as intelligence primarily stems from the populace, it is inevitable that counterinsurgents and insurgents will battle fiercely to gain public support. Therefore, counterinsurgents seek to isolate insurgents from the populace.[28] According to O'Neill, there are two types of public support: passive and active support. Passive support means aid to insurgents through information acquired from people who quietly sympathize with them, while active support means that someone helps insurgents by providing safe havens, serving as liaison agents, and committing acts of civil disobedience.[29] Regardless of the type of support, it is of utmost importance to prevent insurgents from acquiring intelligence from the public. The key prescriptions are to protect the public security and address citizens' grievances so that counterinsurgents can win the hearts and minds of the people.[30]

---

[27] David Galula, *Counterinsurgency Warfare: Theory and Practice* (Westport, Connecticut: Praeger Security International, 2006), 4.

[28] David Kilcullen, *Counterinsurgency* (New York: Oxford University Press, 2010), 10.

[29] Bard E. O'Neill, 94-96.

[30] David Kilcullen, 81-85.

South Korea's COIN History

The term insurgency is nothing new for South Koreans. Insurgencies have occurred regularly as part of the operating environment on the Korean Peninsula since ancient times. In fact, there have been numerous insurgencies related to political, social, religious, and ideological issues throughout Korean history. This section briefly describes four selected insurgencies that occurred for different reasons in different dynasties. These historical cases demonstrate the root causes of insurgency and how they influenced the subsequent events in Korean history.

The first case illustrates a conspiratorial approach linked to strife between different lineages of the royal classes. In Korea's ancient dynasty, bloodlines and relationships, both by family and position, to the political system determined the entire social power structure. As such, a person's position was decided even before birth, on the basis of heredity and occupation, for example, civil officials, soldiers, clerical workers, and artisans.[31] In the Unified Silla dynasty of the early ninth century, Kim Heon-chang, a provincial governor, led an insurgency for the construction of a new country, largely in response to the aristocratic rank system in the Silla dynasty. This system, called the bone rank system, was divided into three layers of sacred bone, true bone, and the head ranks on the basis of heredity.[32] Kim Heon-chang, with true bone status in the Unified Silla aristocratic class, was a direct descendant of King Muyeol, the 29th king of the Korean ancient kingdom of Silla. Kim's father, Kim Ju-won, was supposed to take the throne as the closest relative of the Unified Silla 37th King Seondeok, because the king did not have a son. However, Kim Kyong-sin also from true bone, seized power by force. Kim Ju-won later fled to today's Gangneung area. In 822, his son, Kim Heon-chang led a revolt aiming to regain the

---

[31] Mary E. Corner, *The Koreas*, (California: Abc-Clico, 2009), 180.

[32] Woo-Keun Han, *The History of Korea*, (Seoul: The Eul-Yoo Publishing Company, 1970), 113.

power that Kim Kyong-sin had denied his father.[33] He temporarily gained control over much of Chungcheong, Jeolla, and Gyeongsang provinces, currently located in the southern part of South Korea. However, the royal army succeeded in the counterinsurgency and secured these southern and western areas. This incident caused by political struggle and contradictions of the social class system weakened the ties of the true bone aristocratic class in the Silla dynasty's bone rank system. [34]

The second case represents a military-focused approach related to a conflict between civil and military officials that occurred in the 12th century. The Goryo dynasty had favored scholar-class officials whom were seen as superior to the military-class generals after King Mokjong implemented a policy of putting the military under civil control in 998.[35] The policy made military officers disgruntled, since they were regarded as an inferior class to other aristocratic classes and were even treated as servants of civil officials.[36] Military officials often received insults from civil officers. There was a failed military coup led by Kang cho in 1014, and two other incidents occurred between 1167 and 1170.[37] These failures intensified the anger of the military official groups. In 1167, a young civil administrator humiliated a respected general, Jeong Jung-bu, by burning his long beard with a candle during a royal banquet. When King Uijong held a martial arts competition in 1170, civil administrators forced a late-fifties general, Lee So-eung, to fight with a young champion. When the old general fell to the ground, a young civil official insulted him and even slapped him on the face in front of the king and other fellow military officers. This incident ignited the anger of military officers and caused them to massacre

---

[33] Andrew C. Nahm, *A History of the Korean People: Tradition and Transformation*, (Seoul: Hollym International Corp., 1988), 54.

[34] Woo-Keun Han, 112.

[35] Ibid., 131.

[36] Andrew C. Nahm, 86.

[37] Woo-Keun Han, 140.

many civil officials. As a result, military power groups seized control of the country by the end of the 12th century.[38]

The third case demonstrates a protracted approach related to the complex reasons that drive political, religious, and social issues. It was called the Donghak Peasant Movement led by the peasant class protesting political corruption, the feudal system, and foreign influence on the Peninsula.[39] Throughout the 1800s, Korean peasants suffered from drought and floods that alternately struck the rice fields and farms of Korea. In addition, as the number of upper-class Yangban increased, the manual labor burden increasingly fell upon the peasants. Corrupt governors imposed increased taxes and unpaid labor on the starving farmers. It was provincial governor Jo Byong-gap's tyranny and corruption in Go-bu that ignited the Peasant Insurgency led by Jeon Bong-jun in 1894.[40] The insurgency began with the purpose of reforming the corrupt government and improving living conditions of the peasant. With the increased power of the Donghaks, the government requested the Qing dynasty to assist in quelling the insurgency. Qing sent troops to Joseon; Japan also dispatched troops, citing China's violation of the Convention of Tientsin, which led to the Sino-Japanese War on July 23, 1894.[41] Japan's victory in the war resulted in its intervention in Joseon's domestic politics, which triggered further insurgency on the Peninsula. Although the poorly armed peasants conducted a continuous insurgency by moving to various bases, the Donghaks were crushed by the government, which was supported by the Japanese Army.

The fourth case describes an identity-focused approach related to ideological conflicts. It is South Korea's COIN campaign against a communist-led uprising that occurred in 1948 on

---

[38] Ibid., 156-157

[39] In the 1860s, it arose as a negation to the growing foreign influence in the Joseon Dynasty. There were several clashes involving the Americans and the French. The Joseon Dynasty opened the door to the West with the treaty of Ganghwa in 1876.

[40] Woo-Keun Han, 406-407.

[41] Ibid., 411.

Cheju Island, the largest island in the southernmost part of South Korea. Local insurgents had taken advantage of favorable conditions, primarily a lack of security forces, to use violence to instill fear in the population. The insurgency in Cheju-do had been sustained by support from North Korean communists who were attempting to gain control of the remote islands and create unrest in the South. The campaign led to the death of an estimated 30,000 people and expanded guerrilla warfare to other remote areas and small towns in the mountainous areas of the South.[42] The Cheju-do revolt demonstrated the persistent strength of the South Korean Labor Party (SKLP) to challenge the creation of a new South Korean government by partisan warfare and subversion of the Constabulary.[43] This insurgency, linked to the Korean War, continued until the Korean War armistice became effective in 1953.

South Korea's COIN history provides insight into the root cause of insurgency related to power struggles: conflicts of social classes between civil and military officials; public grievances in terms of combined political, economic, and social problems; and ideology. This research can also shed light on the fundamental reasons why insurgency might happen in North Korea.

Operational Art

The genesis of operational art began in the pursuit of a linkage between tactical and strategic aims. Michael R. Matheny, in *The Roots of Modern American Operational Art,* argues that the Germans were among the first to understand the need for a concept to link strategy with tactics.[44] World War I brought changes to the battlefield due to the expanded battlefield, industrialization, and mass armies.[45] According to Matheny, the armies were so large that military

---

[42] Allan R. Millett, *The War for Korea 1945-1950: A House Burning* (Kansas: The University Press of Kansas, 2005), 142-143.

[43] Ibid., 148

[44] Michael R. Matheny, "The Roots of Modern American Operational Art," http://www.au.af mil/au/awc/awcgate/army-usawc/modern_operations.pdf (accessed 8 October 2011).

[45] Ibid.

experts came to realize that a single tactical success couldn't translate into strategic success and the old framework of strategy and tactics was inadequate to comprehend the modern battlefield. [46]

Soviet military theorists Svechin and Tukhachevsky led the way in developing concepts for the employment of operational art. In 1923 Svechin introduced the term operational art, which was "the totality of maneuvers and battles in a given part of a theater of military action directed toward the achievement of the common goal, set as final in the given period of the campaign."[47] Tukhachevsky recognized that the development of technology required successive and deep operations due to the expansion of the battlefield.[48]

American military planners identified the impact of technology on modern warfare in the interwar period between WW I and WW II. They embraced the operational planning concept linking strategic aims to tactical objectives. However, U.S. operational art did not evolve until the operational level of war was introduced in the 1982 edition of the U.S. Army's Field Manual (FM) 100-5.[49] Shimon Naveh states that the 1986 edition of FM 100-5 was the "perceptional breakthrough" in American recognition of operational art since it "marked the definite recognition of creativity as the basic quality required from operational commanders."[50]

Matheny introduced three levels of war, as described in earlier Leavenworth texts from 1936: the conduct of war, strategy, and tactics.[51] The conduct of war encompasses not only the scope of the armed forces but also political and economic measures, while strategy was defined as

---

[46] Ibid.

[47] Jacob. W. Kipp, *The Evolution of Operational Art: From Napoleon to the Present, The Tsarist and Soviet Operational Art, 1853-1991,* (New York: Oxford, 2011), 64-69.

[48] Ibid. 69-73.

[49] Justin Kelly and Mike Brennan, "Alien: How Operational Art Devoured Strategy," (PA: Strategic Studies Institute, September 2009). http://www.strategicstudiesinstitute.army.mil/pdffiles/pub939.pdf (accessed 8 October 2011).

[50] Shimon Naveh, *In Pursuit of Military Excellence: The Evolution of Operational Theory,* (London: Frank Cass, 1997), 12.

[51] Michael R. Matheny, "The Roots of Modern American Operational Art." Below the description on three levels of war also refers to the same source.

the art of concentrating superior combat power in a theater of war. Tactics was defined as the art of executing strategic movement prior to battle. The United States Army Field Manual 3-0 *Operations* describes the correlation between strategy, operational approach, and tactical actions, and stresses that tactical success is aimed at achieving the strategic objective.[52] In 2011, the U.S. military refined Operational Art in ADP 3-0 as "the pursuit of strategic objectives, in whole or in part, through the arrangement of tactical actions in time, space, and purpose."[53]

To apply operational art to a campaign plan, it would be beneficial for the elements of operational design to serve as a bridge to tactical missions with the strategic end state. In COIN operations, military end state, center of gravity (COG), and a line of effort are important elements. Military end state, according to Joint Publication 5-0, is "a point in time and/or circumstances beyond which the President does not require the military instrument of national power as the primary means to achieve remaining national objectives."[54] Military end state is closely related to strategic aims that should be achieved, making all tactical actions directed toward a final goal. Center of gravity, as defined in JP 5-0, is "a source of power that provides moral or physical strength, freedom of action, or will to act."[55] In COIN operations, it refers to a key object such as the populace or military leadership that highly influences success or failure. As for line of effort, JP 5-0 describes its role as linking multiple tasks and missions using the logic of purpose—cause and effect—to focus efforts toward establishing operational and strategic conditions.[56] A line of effort is critical to planning an operational approach by using the elements of national power in the COIN environment, particularly in the absence of a clear front line. The

---

[52] FM 3-0, 6-1.

[53] U.S. Department of the Army Doctrine Publication 3-0, *Unified Land Operations* (Washington, DC: Headquarters, Department of the Army, 2011), 10.

[54] Joint Publication 5-0, *Joint Operation Planning* (Washington, DC: U.S. Department of Defense 2011), III-4.

[55] Ibid., III-22

[56] Ibid., III-28.

next chapter will show how COIN theory and operational art link to the context of South Korea's COIN operations.

Strategic Context: What Conditions Would the South Be Fighting Under?

Three powerful neighbors, Japan, China, and Russia, as well as the United States, influence the Korean Peninsula geopolitically. Each of these four countries is a major stakeholder in the six-party talks on North Korea's nuclear program along with the two Koreas. In the event that the North Korean regime collapses, each would be involved in resolving the situation. Since Tunisia's protest in December 2010, a series of demonstrations has taken place in the Middle East and North Africa attempting to overthrow brutal dictators. The uprisings spread out across the region, and many were successful in achieving political change. Despite a growing international pro-democracy movement, North Korea's leadership has still maintained a strong grip over the impoverished people. However, the death of Kim Jong-il accelerated the likelihood of North Korea's possible insurgency more than any event since the division of the two Koreas.

Operational Environment

FM 3-0 states that "operational variables describe not only the military aspects of an operational environment but also the population's influence on it. Planners analyze the operational environment in terms of six interrelated operational variables: political, military, economic, social, information, and infrastructure." [57]

The North Korean people have been living under the control of Kim's family for more than 60 years. Kim Il-sung, who founded North Korea in 1948, dominated the country until his death in 1994. His son, Kim Jong-il then inherited supreme power of the regime. Kim Jong-il had maintained the *Juche* ideology of self-reliance created by his father. *Juche* was designed to

---

[57] FM 3-0, 1-5.

establish a monolithic ideological system in North Korea. It was formally adopted as the sole guiding principle for all actions at the 5th Party Congress in 1970.[58] According to *Juche* ideology, there exists no other gods but Kim Il-sung, the country's "Eternal Leader." Such thinking is used as justification for the Kim family's power succession. However, before Kim Jong-il died, signs of political unrest appeared after the official announcement of North Korea's third-generation hereditary succession.[59]

Kim Jong-il's youngest son, Kim Jong-un, is North Korea's new supreme leader. However, as *Juche* ideology is losing its power in North Korean politics, North Korea experts predict that Kim Jong-il's death may cause a fierce power struggle among various factions. These include the ruling clique of conservative hardliners and a group of reformists.[60] There are three crucial issues related to North Korea's power struggle: "divisions over policy, foreign alignments particularly regarding China, and internal power struggles."[61] The division of the Northern leadership may lead to factional infighting, which could be followed by the collapse of North Korea's regime. Furthermore, the fall of the North Korean regime could ignite an insurgency over the entire Korean Peninsula. In this regard, a Northern insurgency might resemble the tribal or sectarian conflicts of Iraq and Afghanistan, and may prove even more difficult for COIN forces to combat.

Just as Mao Zedong argued that "all political power comes from the barrel of a gun," North Korea's military power is the foundation for maintaining the regime and the source of its

---

[58] Jasper Becker, *Rogue Regime: Kim Jong Il and the Looming Threat of North Korea* (New York: Oxford University Press, 2005), 66-67.

[59] Jayshree Bajoria, "North Korea After Kim," Council on Foreign Relations (19 December 2011), http://www.cfr.org/north-korea/north-korea-after-kim/p17322 (accessed 6 April 2012).

[60] The Chosun Ilbo,"Experts Predict Power Struggle When Kim Jong-il Dies," (12 August, 2010), http://english.chosun.com/site/data/html_dir/2010/08/12/2010081200281 html (accessed 19 September 2011).

[61] The telegraph, "Power struggle rages in North Korean regime," (24 September, 2010), http://www.telegraph.co.uk/news/worldnews/asia/northkorea/8022800/Power-struggle-rages-in-North-Korean-regime.html (accessed 19 September 2011).

political power.[62] The North's military has dominated political and economic institutions since Kim Jong-il adopted the Military First Policy as a guideline for domestic governance and foreign policy.[63] The North has used the military as a means of strengthening the Kim family's political power and resolving domestic political instability. In fact, Kim Jong-il emerged as a North Korean political figure through the Blue House raid and the *USS Pueblo* case in 1968.[64] There was North Korea's nuclear crisis in 1993 before the death of Kim Il-Sung. Moreover, provocative nuclear threats in 2009 and the *Cheonan* sinking and the *Yeonpyong* artillery attack in 2010 were deliberately intended to strengthen Kim Jong-un's political position in the process of power succession.[65] The transfer of power was allegedly the cause of these events.

North Korea is armed with nuclear weapons of mass destruction, long-range missiles, more than 1.2 million conventional forces, 5 million reserves, and 200,000 special operations forces. The U.S. Department of State declared in a Background Note on North Korea, "North Korea forces have a substantial numerical advantage over South Korea. The North has one of the world's largest special operations forces, designed for insertion behind the lines in wartime. North Korea's navy is primarily a coastal navy, with antiquated surface and submarine fleets. Its air force has twice the number of aircraft as the South, but, except for a few advanced fighters,

---

[62] Mao Tsetung, *Quotations from Chairman Mao Tsetung* (Peking: Foreign Language Press, 1972), 61.

[63] Alexander V. Vorontsov, "North Korea's Military First Policy: A Curse or a Blessing?" Brookings Institution (26 May, 2006), http://www.brookings.edu/opinions/2006 /0526northkorea_ vorontsov.aspx (accessed 18 September, 2011).

[64] Victor D. Cha, "The Rationale for Enhanced Engagement of North Korea: After the Perry Policy Review," Asian Survey (November/December 1999), http://www.jstor.org/discover/10.2307/ 3021142?uid=3739672&uid=2129&uid=2&uid=70&uid= 4&uid=3739256&sid=56006875803 (accessed 6 April 2012).

[65] U.S. Office of the Director of National Intelligence, "Statement for the Record on the Worldwide Threat Assessment of the U.S. Intelligence Community," (10 February, 2011), http://www.dni.gov/ testimonies/ 20110210_testimony_clapper.pdf (accessed 2 December, 2011).

the North's air force is obsolete."[66] In case of the fall of the North's regime, the most dangerous

scenario South Korea may face would be the North's loss of control over weapons of mass

destruction during a power struggle. Under these circumstances, South Korea's COIN

environment would be even worse than that of Iraq or Afghanistan in terms of the insurgents'

military capability.

North Korea's economy is centrally planned under state management and control. It is a

collectivist economy based on state ownership of the means of production. It also emphasizes

military development. The economic situation began to deteriorate rapidly with the collapse of

the Soviet Union and the introduction of a Chinese market economy in the 1990s. After the death

of Kim Il-sung in 1994, the inefficiencies of North Korea's central economic planning system

pushed the economy into crisis with rising inflation and a thriving black market. Flood and

drought, starting in the 1980s, resulted in widespread famine and starvation for the population of

North Korea. The North's residents still suffer from prolonged malnutrition and poor living

conditions. The regime began to allow farmers to run private markets on an experimental basis in

an effort to increase agricultural production in 2002, but it withdrew its permission for the new

policy in 2005. As a result, complaints by the North Korean people continue to increase.[67]

North Korea depends heavily on sales of military equipment and the illegal drug trade

abroad for its foreign currency income. A U.S. congressional report on the North Korean

economy stated that "North Korea is thought to have sold hundreds of ballistic missiles to Iran,

Iraq, Syria, Pakistan, and other nations in the past decade to earn foreign currency. It is earning

between $500 million and $1 billion annually from the narcotics trade. North Korea is thought to

produce more than 40 tons of opium per year, which would make it the world's third-largest

---

[66] U.S. Department of State, "Background Note: North Korea," (29 April, 2011), http://www.state.gov/r/pa/ei/bgn/2792 htm (accessed 18 September, 2011).

[67] Jasper Becker, 36.

opium exporter and sixth-largest heroin exporter."[68] After the international community took

measures against the regime's illicit financial activities, the North's economy began to suffer.

Despite that, North Korea still spends resources needed for civilian consumption on its military

build-up. Under these circumstances, the regime's inefficient economic system could spur

domestic unrest.

North Korea's economic problems have extended to social issues. The regime's strong

control no longer frightens citizens at the crossroads of life and death. As the North loses control

over its population, the illegal drug trade is becoming prevalent among ordinary citizens. The

rules of money and power are also becoming commonplace rather than the rule of laws and

regulations. While the North's officials bend the rules to make life better for themselves and their

families, the regime becomes a corrupt society that relies on bribery. Moreover, diverse social

problems such as drug trafficking, robbery, murder, and prostitution are growing in North Korea.

In particular, drug trafficking is a serious condition in the cities adjoining the Chinese border,

such as Hoiryeong, Musan, and Sinuiju. This drug problem could damage the character of the

North Korean people and further the expansion of criminal organizations and illegal armed

forces.[69]

In addition, North Korea is notorious for its consistent disregard for basic human rights.

The U.S. Department of State describes human rights in North Korea in a Background Note:

"Reported human rights abuses include arbitrary and lengthy imprisonment, torture and degrading

treatment, poor prison conditions, forced labor, public executions, prohibitions or severe

restrictions on freedom of speech, the press, movement, assembly, religion, and privacy, denial of

---

[68] Dick K. Nanto, "The North Korean Economy: Overview and Policy Analysis," CRS Report for Congress (18 April, 2007) http://www.nautilus.org/publications/essays/napsnet/reports/07045CRS.pdf (accessed 27 September).

[69] Mattew Clayton, "Drugs in the DPRK2006-2011: A Quantitative Analysis," NK News (March 2012), http://nknews.org/wp-content/uploads/2012/03/Comparative-Analysis-on-DPRK-Drugs.pdf (accessed 6 April 2012).

the right of citizens to change their government, and suppression of workers' rights."[70] In North Korea, it is very common to downplay and violate human rights. Social problems such as drug trafficking, corruption, and human rights violations contribute to public grievances, which are a primary root cause of insurgency. Criminal organizations often link themselves to insurgencies.

The privacy of the population is heavily controlled by the authorities, while all sources of information, such as radio and television, are strictly censored by the government. In addition, the regime prohibits access to foreign books and newspapers in order to prevent the spread of the capitalist culture inside North Korea. The public radio frequency is also fixed to central broadcasting. Cellular phone access is limited to an internal network, while Internet use is limited to the political elite. A crackdown on means of communication is being ramped up to further block the free flow of information. Nevertheless, Northern residents are using the Internet and mobile phones in a variety of ways, outside the control of the government.[71] North Korea's infrastructure is aging and in need of a wide range of maintenance and new construction. The regime's limited and unpaved road system is estimated at 20,000 to 31,200 kilometers, while the railway network covers only 5,000-kilometers.[72] Only a few of the 12 ports can handle large ships, while only 22 of the 49 airports have paved runways. The North produces 34 percent of its electricity from fossil fuel and 65.6 percent using hydroelectric power generators. [73]

---

[70] U.S. Department of State, "Background Note: North Korea."

[71] Peter Nesbitt, "Joint U.S.-Korea Academic Studies: Emerging Voice," Korea Economic Institute (2011 Special Edition), http://www.keia.org/sites/default/files/publications/emergingvoices _final_peternesbitt.pdf (accessed 6 April 2012).

[72] Encyclopedia of the Nations, "Korea, North-Infrastructure, power, and communications," http://www.nationsencyclopedia.com/economies/Asia-and-the-Pacific/Korea-North-INFRASTRUCTURE-POWER-AND-COMMUNICATIONS html (accessed 27 September, 2011).

[73] Ibid.

Character of North Korea's Military

North Korea's past provocations exemplify how much North Korea relied on physical violence to create an unstable condition on the Korean Peninsula. The North has been responsible for almost all terrorism-related acts against the Korean people since 1958.[74] The most common types of terrorist tactics used against South Korea have included bombing, shooting, and hijacking.[75] Another aspect of the North's physical violence is guerrilla infiltration.[76] A guerrilla incursion occurred in 1968 in Uljin and Samchuck, located in the eastern regions of South Korea. Approximately 120 North Korean special agents secretly infiltrated the regions to conduct a guerilla war. In 1996, a North Korean submarine infiltrated Gangneung, located on the east coast of South Korea, with the purpose of gaining information.

North Korea's possession of weapons of mass destruction (WMDs) has been a matter of significant concern to the international community. The North has conducted missile tests, triggering anxiety in the Pacific region as well as on the Peninsula. No Dong ballistic missiles, with a range of 870 miles, have the capability to strike South Korea, Japan, and various Pacific countries. North Korea is also believed to have enough plutonium for approximately eight nuclear weapons. Mark Fitzpatrick, director of the non-proliferation and disarmament program at the International Institute for Strategic Studies, stated that "Pyongyang may also have a submarine capable of launching a suicide nuclear attack."[77]

---

[74] See Joohoon Kim,"Current Issues Concerning Korea's Anti-Terrorism Programs," Master of Military Art and Science Thesis (Command and General Staff College, 2010), 31-32. Below terrorism related descriptions are referred to the same source.

[75] Ibid.

[76] Office of The Korea Chair, "Record of North Korea's Major Conventional Provocations since 1960s," Center for Strategic and International Studies (May 25 2010), http://csis.org/files/publication/ 100525_ North_Koreas_ Provocations.pdf (accessed 27 September 2011).

[77] Luke Harding, "After Kim Jong-il's death, what will happen to North Korea's nuclear arsenal?", the guardian, http://www.guardian.co.uk/world/2011/dec/19/north-korea-nuclear-arsenal-dangers (accessed 7 January 2012).

In addition, a potential Northern insurgency can employ the Improvised Explosive Device (IED) tactics used by Iraqi and Afghanistan insurgents. General Walter Sharp, former U.S. Forces Korea commander, stressed that U.S. Forces in Korea should prepare for any Iraq-style insurgency tactics that might be used by North Korea in a conflict on the Korean Peninsula.[78]

Preparation Is Essential

The PMESII (Political, Military, Economic, Social, Information, and Infrastructure) analysis helps us to understand the level of complexity inherent in North Korea's various problems and to identify the factors that may contribute to the rise of an insurgency. Countries with political unrest, severe economic hardship, and social inequalities are more susceptible to military coups and revolution.[79] This chapter has demonstrated that North Korea rules its people through the fear of harsh consequences, relying heavily on overwhelming coercion. Decades of the Kim family's exclusive rule and military-first policy have worsened economic and social conditions. Within this context, there is a high possibility of an insurgency that may stem from the public grievances associated with political, economic, and social issues.

As the Northern regime's structure is illegitimate and fragile, it may not properly function once it loses control of the population. PMESII analysis shows that a successful revolt would be likely to incite a mass uprising and have a ripple effect on the expansion of insurgency across North Korea. Therefore, South Korea needs to prepare for such a situation and devise measures to

---

[78] Stars and Stripes, "USFK commander takes war cue from Iraq," (29 June, 2007), http://www.stripes.com/news/usfk-commander-takes-war-cue-from-iraq-1.80485 (accessed 19 September 2011). General Sharp said, "I do believe that North Korea is taking lessons out of Iraq, and they will change and adapt tactics. I greatly worry about IEDs showing up in this theater."

[79] Misagh Parsa, *States, Ideologies, and Social Revolutions* (Cambridge, UK: Cambridge University Press, 2000), 19-25.

address problems on the basis of expected strategy, strategic objectives, and tactics of the North insurgency described above.

Functional Area Analysis (FAA): Required Capabilities

In case of the collapse of the North, the South may face the following complex challenges derived from the interaction of various root causes of the insurgency and strategic context.

- How to control the massive influx of Northern defectors into the South
- When to intervene to avoid chaos or "anarchy" in the North
- How to seize WMDs command and control ahead of an insurgency
- How to deal with a hybrid threat of conventional and unconventional weapons
- How to separate insurgents from the public and gain public support in the North
- How to cope with Chinese external support to insurgents

Understanding the operational environment and the character of the North enables us to predict possible political objectives, strategies, and tactics of a Northern insurgency. The political objective of the insurgents would likely be to throw out Kim Jong-un and his regime and become the leading power in North Korea. If the South and its coalition partners intervene to prevent chaotic disorder that may endanger security on the Peninsula, insurgents might pursue the following strategy:

- Seize, retain, and exploit the initiative through WMDs control
- Bleed South Korea and its coalition partners to exhaustion and force them to withdraw
- Provoke the South and contain coalition partners through external support from China

Thus the South needs to increase its integrated intelligence, surveillance, and reconnaissance (ISR) capability to gain a relative advantage over a Northern insurgency, especially the North's WMDs facilities as well as its conventional capabilities. In addition, it requires military and nonmilitary resources to counter provocative and protracted conflicts that the Northern insurgency would use to exhaust the South. Further, it is significant that South Korea needs the support of coalition partners to cope with Chinese external support, as well as its diplomatic efforts with China.

To achieve strategic objectives, the Northern insurgents might rely heavily on their hybrid capabilities, which would support the following tactics:

- Provocation: execute provocative events against the South in order to cause the South's overreaction and create instability.
- Intimidation: intimidate and kill people who are willing to help the South and its coalition partners in order to prevent the populace from cooperating with counterinsurgents.
- Protraction: prolong the conflict in order to exhaust the South and its partners, erode their political will, and weaken their public support.
- Exhaustion: impose costs in terms of lives, resources, and political capital in order to convince the South that the war is not worth continuing.[80]

To counter a future Northern insurgency's tactics, it is necessary to use a combination of offensive and defensive operations. However, neither of these operations alone guarantees success in COIN. Nonmilitary elements can often be more effective components than military means to address the root causes of insurgency because COIN is a battle for gaining public support. And public support often depends on honest, up-to-date information to counter the insurgents' propaganda. Further, military actions alone can't achieve the COIN goal of "winning the hearts and minds of the population." While the South needs a military-centric approach to eliminate WMDs and cope with guerrilla and terrorism tactics, including IED attacks, it also needs a population-centric approach to address public grievances and isolate the populace from the insurgents.

U.S. Army Doctrine Publication (ADP) 3-0, *Unified Land Operations*, describes the foundations of unified land operations as initiative, decisive action, army core competencies, and mission command.[81] To seize, retain, and exploit the initiative, the South's counterinsurgents would need to degrade the coherence of the North through the simultaneous combination of

---

[80] David Kilcullen, *The Accidental Guerrilla* (New York: Oxford University Press, 2009), 30-32. Kilcullen describes four al Qa'ida's tactics as provocation, intimidation, protraction, and exhaustion. These tactics are applicable to tactics that the Northern insurgency may pursue despite a different strategic context.

[81] ADP 3-0. 5-6.

offensive, defensive, and stability operations against a Northern insurgency with both conventional and hybrid threats.[82] Thus, combined arms maneuver and wide area security, described as U.S. Army core competencies in ADP 3-0, are helpful in defeating enemy forces and protecting populations, forces, and infrastructure.[83] In addition, mission command is required to empower agile and adaptive leaders who can anticipate and adapt quickly to changing conditions in a fluid mix of offensive, defensive, and stability operations.[84]

Functional Needs Analysis (FNA): Capability Gaps

Following the 1953 armistice, South Korea continued to focus almost exclusively on conventional warfare in preparation for a North Korean invasion. However, the South has been more exposed to North Korea's numerous guerrilla attacks and terrorism. Within this context, the South has sought to strengthen its domestic counter-guerrilla and counter-terrorism capacity. In 1982, the South Korean government established a national emergency program for guerrilla- and terrorism-related events with the passage of the Presidential Order for Counterterrorism.[85] The South Korean military accumulated its COIN experience in Vietnam, waging unconventional warfare against the Viet Cong. Since the South's military launched peacekeeping operations in Somalia in 1993, it has become one of the major contributing nations to international peacekeeping. South Korea's participation in Iraq and Afghanistan after 9/11 has built up its potential COIN capability in terms of stability operations. Thus, the South has the following current capabilities:

- Conventional warfare capability combined with U.S. Forces in Korea
- Counter-guerrilla and counter-terrorism capability against North Korean provocation
- COIN experience in the Korean War and the Vietnam War

---

[82] Ibid., 5.

[83] Ibid., 6.

[84] Ibid.

[85] See Joohoon Kim, "Current Issues Concerning Korea's Anti-Terrorism Programs."

- Stability operations experience in Iraq and Afghanistan and peace operations.

Despite these capabilities, the South Korean Army lacks the synthesis of diverse capabilities and experience needed to conduct COIN operations appropriate to the mission and environment on the Korean Peninsula. South Korea has had COIN experiences throughout its history, but it has failed to establish an institutionalized memory reflecting COIN principles in its military doctrine. It neglected to reflect sufficiently on the valuable lessons learned from its experience in Vietnam as well as its history of counter-guerrilla and counter-terrorism against the North.

John Nagl, in his book *Learning to Eat Soup with a Knife*, points out that the U.S. in Vietnam and the British military in Malaya sought different approaches in terms of the organizational learning culture.[86] He says that the British tried to adjust failing policies and strategy, while the U.S. military tended to overlook the importance of adaptation such as fitting the military size and organization into a given environment.[87] In fact, a strong belief in the critical essence of the defeat of a conventional enemy in Vietnam turned out to be an obstacle to the U.S. military's own policy of "Learn and Adapt."[88] In this regard, it is a weakness in the organizational learning culture for "Learn and Adapt" that causes the most significant gap between current and desired capabilities. Thus the South needs to create an organizational learning culture to adapt rapidly to the challenges it may face in the strategic contexts.

Of facing an insurgency, Sir Robert Thomson wrote, "The government must have an overall plan. This plan must cover not just the security measures and military operations. It must include all political, social, economic, administrative, police and other measures which have a bearing on the insurgency. Above all it must clearly define roles and responsibilities to avoid

---

[86] John A Nagl, *Learning to Eat Soup with a Knife: Counterinsurgency Lessons from Malaya and Vietnam* (Chicago: The University of Chicago Press, 2005), 191-208.

[87] Ibid.

[88] Ibid., 220-223. FM 3-24 describes "Learn and Adapt" as a modern COIN imperative.

duplication of effort and to ensure that there are no gaps in the government's field of action."[89]

The Northern insurgency's military, political, economic, and social context precludes military forces alone from countering insurgency as a solitary contributor in the complex and extremely challenging environment South Korea might face. Eliminating the insurgents' violence and protecting the people are the primary missions for COIN forces. Winning the hearts and minds of the population as well as defeating the insurgency is critical to success in COIN. Within this context, the South's conventional military alone is not sufficient to address a potential North Korean insurgency based on the North's protracted, complex, and ambiguous approaches. Thus efforts by the entire government are required to eliminate the various root causes through a proper balance of military and civil efforts.

Given that the nature of the COIN environment is complex and ambiguous, the most important factors for COIN success are information and time. As adaptive insurgents with initial operational initiatives decide when, where, and how they fight, denying information to counterinsurgents, it is important for counterinsurgents to acquire the information necessary to react quickly. Moreover, as the Northern military's guerrilla warfare and terrorism may be primary tactics, the roles of small-unit leaders on the ground would be critical factors to successful COIN operations in terms of time-sensitive decision making.

Functional Solutions Analysis (FSA): Gap-Filling Solutions

With some of the potential challenges now identified, the monograph will examine potential doctrine, organization, and leadership and education solutions of the DOTMLPF that can affect counterinsurgency requirements for South Korea. In the area of doctrine, this examination specifically addresses the value of incorporating operational art and design into the South's doctrinal constructs. In the area of organizational solutions, the monograph studies

---

[89] Sir Robert Thompson, *Defeating Communist Insurgency* (St. Petersburg Florida: Hailer Publishing, 1966 republished 2005), 55.

implementation of a "whole-of-government" approach for unity of effort between armed services and other agencies. Finally, the leadership and education aspect focuses on the application of mission command.

Doctrine: Operational Art and Design

Clausewitz points out, "War has its own grammar, but not its own logic."[90] In South Korea's COIN, logic refers to immutable political intent that counterinsurgents and insurgents pursue, while grammar indicates mutable ways and means to achieve political intent on both sides. In this regard, it is important to understand the relation of the military to national policy for achieving strategic goals. Insurgency, by definition, intends to achieve political aims through tactical actions. Thus South Korea needs to present a clear political objective so that military forces can seek strategic aims by arranging tactical actions that fit into time, space, and purpose.

Clausewitz also postulates that nations go to war for one logical reason: "to perform an act of force to compel our enemy to do our will."[91] North Korea's insurgency will attempt to achieve its strategic objectives of preventing reunification and building its new leadership through the linkage of diverse tactical actions. Northern insurgents are likely to expand the insurgency campaign from the North into the South by using their tactics of provocation, intimidation, protraction, and exhaustion. Within this context, there is a possibility for the North to attack an isolated island, perhaps in the Yeonpyeong Islands located in the west sea near the border with the North, to gain an upper hand in terms of strategic initiative. Further, the Northern insurgency may capitalize on external support from China to overcome its relative weakness in terms of material and non-material resources. To efficiently react to such a diverse scenario, the South will need concerted civil and military effort, as well as joint and multinational operations. Moreover,

---

[90] Carl von Clausewitz, *On War*, edited and translated by Michael Howard and Peter Paret (Princeton NJ: Princeton University Press, 1984), 605-612.

[91] Ibid., 75.

it is important to isolate individual elements within the insurgency system from each other to deter the effect of synchronization. However, what matters most is achieving strategic aims through the efficient arrangement of tactical actions, rather than winning a series of separate victories on the tactical level.

Gaddis warns planners not to seek a solution from singular causes or independent variables, but to seek a solution interrelated to variables.[92] Without directing strategic objectives, independent victories at tactical levels do not necessarily translate into success at strategic levels. Thus it is necessary for counterinsurgents to look a few steps ahead, beyond the battle itself.[93] Shimon Naveh, *In Pursuit of Military Excellence*, defines operational art as "the intermediated area between tactics and strategy."[94] The levels of war correlate to specific levels of planning, and they help organize thought and approaches to a problem. [95] Therefore successful counterinsurgency depends largely upon an effective application of operational art for linking strategic levels and tactical levels, which will lead to desired success at national levels.

To cope with unpredictable and complex challenges that lie ahead, the South Korean Army also needs to consider the application of design methodology. Design, as defined in FM 5-0 *The Operations Process,* is "a methodology for applying critical and creative thinking to understand, visualize, and describe complex, ill-structured problems and develop approaches to solve them."[96] The South Korean Army currently uses the Military Decision Making Process (MDMP) to plan operations and to execute conventional warfare in the case of open hostilities on

---

[92] John Lewis Gaddis, *The Landscape of History: How Historians Map the Past* (New York: Oxford University Press, 2002), 61.

[93] Michael R. Matheny, "The Roots of Modern American Operational Art," http://www.au.af mil/au/awc/awcgate/army-usawc/modern_operations.pdf (accessed 8 October, 2011).

[94] Shimon Naveh, *In Pursuit of Military Excellence: The Evolution of Operational Theory* (London: Frank Cass, 1997), 41.

[95] FM 3-0, 6-1.

[96] FM 5-0, *The Operations Process* (Washington, D.C.: Department of the Army, 2010), 3-1.

the Korean Peninsula. Addressing conventional threats is a relatively well-structured problem because the South has prepared for this type of war since the division of the two Koreas and is well aware of operational environment, problems, and operational approach.

Conversely, the South's COIN operations require an understanding of ill-structured problems gained by applying their knowledge, experience, and insight. Bryan Lawson, the author of *How Designers Think*, argues that "design is as much a matter of finding problems as it is of solving them."[97] He stresses the importance of identifying problems to avoid an unnecessary iterative process from formulating to moving. South Korea also needs a creative and adaptive approach to reduce uncertainty and chaos in order to cope with the Northern insurgency.[98] Because both the insurgents and the counterinsurgents will seek to win the hearts and minds of the public, it is important to create a unique approach that makes the two sides' approaches different. This requires creative thinking, which will lead to outmaneuvering the enemy. Thus, the problem South Korea should solve is 'how to win the hearts and minds ahead of insurgents,' rather than just 'winning the hearts and minds of the public.' The former means 'how to gain a relative advantage over the enemy,' while the latter means 'how to go my own way as planned regardless of the enemy.'

As war is a matter of two conflicting opponents or opposing wills, the first reciprocal approach is more appropriate, although it makes a situation more unpredictable. In particular, both sides will struggle to predict the result of conflicts between the two sides' unique approaches, trying to stay ahead of each other. In addition, ill-structured problems derive from the 'no front' character of COIN operations, unlike major operations that have clear fronts. Conventional warfare is like a competition on a designated track between two runners, while unconventional or

---

[97] Bryan Lawson, *How Designers Think* (Boston: Architectural Press, 2006), 117.

[98] Antoine Bousquet, *The Scientific Way of Warfare* (New York: Columbia University Press, 2009), 3-4.

hybrid warfare is a competition over a route that is not designated, so that speed is not necessarily a decisive factor. Thus designers need to rely on creative thinking more than planners who mostly develop a well-structured plan on the basis of a pre-planned Operations Plan (OPLAN) or Standing Operation Procedure (SOP).

The South Korean military thus needs to apply design methodology to COIN and educate military designers in its potential application. They can then create unique approaches to outmaneuver a North Korean insurgency and win popular support. Given the complexity of the COIN environment, design methodology is necessary to avoid an unnecessary iterative process that involves formulating problems and setting corrective action in motion while complementing the role of MDMP in the planning process. Therefore, operational art and design methodology will fill a doctrinal gap and lead to strategic success in COIN operations.

Organization: Unity of Effort

Unity of effort is coordination and cooperation among all military forces and other organizations toward a commonly recognized objective, even if the forces and nonmilitary organizations are not necessarily part of the same command structure.[99] To recognize the importance of unity of effort, it is necessary to seek an understanding of the role of military and civil measures. Kilcullen argues that "the role of military forces is to dominate the environment and reduce the energy in the insurgency, taking it 'off boil' to allow the other elements of national power to become effective."[100] At the early stage of North Korea's insurgency, the most urgent military efforts would be to prevent the Northern insurgency's expansion into major operations that might result in great human and material losses. Military efforts are effective only when

---

[99] FM 6-0, *Mission Command: Command and Control of Army Forces* (Washington, D.C.: Department of the Army, 2003), 2-7.

[100] David Kilcullen, "Countering Global Insurgency," (30 November 2004) http://smallwarsjournal. com/documents/kilcullen.pdf (accessed December 3 2011).

integrated into a comprehensive government approach including various elements of national power in a complex COIN environment. The realization that combined use of national elements is critical to COIN success enables us to understand the need for unity of effort between the military and civilian components of the government. Civilian programs can help address the root causes of insurgency and meet the North Korean people's needs, which will result in gaining the people's allegiance. Moreover, civil measures in conjunction with military efforts would contribute to undermining an insurgency and isolating the Northern insurgents from the population. Military efforts would help prevent the North's provocations and protect the population from the insurgents.

Kilcullen points out that unity of effort can be achieved through "a common strategic understanding and a common best practice."[101] A common strategic understanding allows us to pursue strategic objectives, while a common best practice leads to tactical success. Hoffman argues that a comprehensive COIN needs "a clear strategy, a defined structure for implementing it, and a vision for inter-government agency cooperation and the unified effort to guide it."[102] In this regard, South Korea needs to consider a lead agency that could leverage an interagency unity of effort. Kalev I. Sepp, in his article "Best Practices in Counterinsurgency," stated that "a government needs a single, fully empowered executive to direct and coordinate counterinsurgency efforts. Power sharing among political bodies, while appropriate and necessary in peacetime, presents wartime vulnerabilities and gaps in coordination that insurgents can

---

[101] Ibid.

[102] Bruce Hoffman, "Combating Al Qaeda and the Militant Islamic Threat" Testimony presented to the House Armed Services Committee, Subcommittee on Terrorism, Unconventional Threats and Capabilities (February 16, 2006), http://www.rand.org/pubs/testimonies/2006/RAND_CT255.pdf (accessed 3 December 2011)

exploit."[103] Therefore South Korea needs a leading organization to coordinate efforts to leverage all elements of national power.

Leadership and Education: Mission Command

ADP 3-0 *Unified Land Operations* defines mission command as "the exercise of authority and direction by the commander using mission orders to enable disciplined initiative within the commander's intent to empower agile and adaptive leaders in the conduct of unified land operations."[104] Martin Van Creveld, the author of *Command in War*, argues that "the fundamentals of command in conventional war may require modification, even inversion, in a counterinsurgency environment where purely military factors are less important than psychological and political ones."[105] A challenge that the South Korean Army may face in an uncertain environment is being confronted with hybrid threats that characterize combinations of regular and irregular groups. In particular, an insurgency or terrorism where there is no clear front will increase uncertainty due to lack of information, which would make it difficult to respond to a situation quickly. FM 3-24 *Counterinsurgency* states that Mission Command is ideally suited to the mosaic nature of COIN operations, as leaders at lower units better understand a situation on the ground and can make a decision properly.[106]

Van Creveld also states that an organization may react in either of two ways to carry out a mission when the information available is less than needed to perform the mission: One is to increase its information-processing capacity; the other is to design tasks that enable it to operate

---

[103] Kalev I. Sepp, "Best Practices in Counterinsurgency," Military Review (May-June 2005), http://www.au.af mil/au/awc/awcgate/milreview/sepp.pdf (accessed 27 July 2011).

[104] ADP 3-0, 6.

[105] Martin Van Creveld, *Command in War* (Massachusetts: Harvard University Press, 1985), 262.

[106] FM 3-24, 1-2.

on the basis of less information.[107] FM 6-0 describes two solutions for reducing uncertainty: an information-focused solution and an action-focused solution.[108] While the first tends to focus on processing more information at the higher units, the latter allows subordinates to delegate authority to the lower units that can deal with the information. The information-focused approach increases uncertainty at lower units, but an action-focused one enables subordinate units to make decisions on their own and offer flexibility and agility. Thus the South needs to decentralize capabilities and operations in order to effectively counter decentralized insurgents by reducing the amount of data processing required. Helmuth von Moltke, Chief of the Prussian General Staff in 1857, applied the mission-oriented command system stressing decentralized initiative within an overall strategic design. He based his choice on understanding that the command method encourages the initiative of subordinates and facilitates effective tactical operations under mission command.[109] Mission command grants freedom for subordinate leaders at all levels to exercise disciplined initiative within the commander's intent to outmaneuver the insurgents in cognitive and physical space.

Conclusions

This monograph described a common conceptual understanding of COIN theory and doctrine and South Korea's COIN imperatives using a capability-based assessment. Through analysis of the strategic context, it identified the necessity of preparation for COIN in case of a collapse in the North. Functional Area Analysis (FAA) illustrated the required capability, while Functional Need Analysis (FNA) identified the capability gap. Functional Solution Analysis (FSA) provided broad 'gap-filling solutions.' It is important to create a learning organization and a culture that promotes the learning of operational art, unity of effort, and mission command to

---

[107] Martin Van Creveld, 269.

[108] FM 6-0, 1-11.

[109] Ibid., 1-15.

succeed in COIN operations and adapt to a complex and complicated COIN environment. The South Korean Army also needs to devote time and effort to developing a new COIN doctrine suited to the COIN environment it may face. In addition, it needs to consider reorganizing the appropriate force structure in preparation for COIN operations while maintaining current conventional warfare approaches in the face of North Korea's hybrid threats.

Since the Korean War, the South Korean Army has been playing a significant role in both conventional and unconventional operations. General Sir Rupert Smith states that future wars will be war among the people, and they will fight in an ill-defined operational environment.[110] COIN operations will be more army-centric and rely less on other services because they deal with interaction between people and territorially centered operations. In this regard, the Army in South Korea will be the primary arm of the COIN forces, in keeping with COIN's principles of the population primacy. Therefore, the South's Army needs an understanding of operational art and design that will enable it to link strategy and tactics and address ill-structured problems through creative and critical thinking. The Korean Army also should recognize its role as part of the government's all-encompassing approach so that it can achieve unity of effort. This comprehensive approach, combining all elements of national power, is paramount to success. Moreover, the Army needs to decentralize command authority to outmaneuver the insurgents through operational adaptability.

What follows is a recommendation for the successful execution of COIN operations on the peninsula. Operational thinking, as defined in *Systems Thinking*, is "an ingenious way to overcome the difficulties encountered in constructing and simulating complex mental models."[111] 'An ingenious way' stems from contemplating the possibility of events beforehand. T.E.

---

[110] General Sir Rupert Smith, *The Utility of Force: The Art of War in the Modern World* (London: Allen Lane, The Penguin Group, 2005), 372.

[111] Jamshid Gharajedaghi, *Systems Thinking: Managing Chaos and Complexity: A Platform for Designing Business Architecture* (New York: Elsevier, 2006), 118.

Lawrence, known as 'Lawrence of Arabia,' reduced the extent of uncertain dimensions and framed the environmental problem through operational thinking during World War I. Lawrence's effort to anticipate future events enabled him to later react properly to the Turks by outmaneuvering them in cognitive space. Milan Vego, in *Operational Warfare at Sea*, defines the term operational thinking as "thinking broadly and far ahead of the current events."[112] Operational thinking would enable the South Korean Army to respond quickly and seize the initiative in COIN operations.

This monograph describes a Doctrine, Organization, and Leadership and Education solution approach to mitigate the gaps between the current capability and needed capability. The realization of these three elements is critical to success in the South's COIN; it should be followed by the South's review of Training, Material, Personnel, and Facility solution approaches. Training should emphasize a seamless transition from combined arms maneuver to wide area security. Material requirements should include considerations such as budgets and equipment required in COIN operations, along with the non-military aspects in concert with government organizations. In addition, COIN experts who will play a significant role in COIN operations need to be better educated. Training sites and facilities for COIN operations should also be developed to build a better base of knowledge for the South Korean military to execute COIN operations.

---

[112] Milan Vego, *Operational Warfare at Sea: Theory and Practice* (New York: Routledge, 2010), 202.

BIBLIOGRAPHY

Books

Becker, Jasper. *Rogue Regime: Kim Jong Il and The Looming Threat of North Korea.* New York: Oxford University Press, 2005.

Bousquet, Antoine. *The Scientific Way of Warfare.* New York: Columbia University Press, 2009.

Creveld, Martin Van. *Command in War.* Massachusetts: Harvard University Press, 1985.

Clausewitz, Carl von. *On War*, edited and translated by Michael Howard and Peter Paret Princeton NJ: Princeton University Press, 1984.

Corner, Mary E. *The Koreas.* California: Abc-Clico, 180.

Gaddis, John Lewis. *The Landscape of History: How Historians Map the Past.* New York: Oxford University Press, 2002.

Galula, David. *Counterinsurgency Warfare: Theory and Practice.* Westport, Connecticut: Praeger Security International, 2006.

Gharajedaghi, Jamshid. *Systems Thinking: Managing Chaos and Complexity: A Platform for Designing Business Architecture.* New York: Elsevier, 2005.

Han, Woo-Keun. *The History of Korea.* Seoul: The Eul-Yoo Publishing Company, 1970.

Kilcullen, David. *Counterinsurgency.* New York: Oxford University Press, 2010.

Kilcullen, David. *The Accidental Guerrilla.* New York: Oxford University Press, 2009.

Kipp, Jacob. *The Evolution of Operational Art: From Napoleon to the Present, The Tsarist and Soviet Operational Art 1853-1991.* New York: Oxford, 2011.

Lawson, Bryan. *How Designers Think.* Boston: Architectural Press, 2006.

Millett, Allan R. *The War for Korea 1945-1950: A House Burning.* Kansas: The University Press of Kansas, 2005.

Nagl, John A. *Learning to Eat Soup with a Knife: Counterinsurgency Lessons from Malaya and Vietnam.* Chicago: University of Chicago Press, 2002.

Nahm, Andrew C. *A History of the Korean People: Tradition and Transformation.* Seoul: Hollym International Corp., 1988.

Naveh, Shimon. *In Pursuit of Military Excellence: The Evolution of Operational Theory.* London: Frank Cass, 1997.

O'Neill, Bard E. *Insurgency and Terrorism: From Revolution to Apocalypse.* Dulles VA: Potomac Book, 2005.

Parsa, Misagh. *States, Ideologies, and Social Revolutions.* Cambridge, UK: Cambridge University Press, 2000.

Record, Jeffrey. *Beating Goliath: Why Insurgencies Win.* Washington D.C.: Potomac Books, 2009.

Smith, Rupert. *The Utility of Force: The Art of War in the Modern World.* London: The Penguin Group, 2005.

Thompson, Robert. *Defeating Communist Insurgency.* St. Petersburg Florida: Hailer Publishing, 2005.

Tsetung, Mao. *Quotations from Chairman Mao Tsetung*. Peking: Foreign Language Press, 1972.

Vego, Milan. *Operational Warfare at Sea: Theory and Practice*. New York: Routledge, 2010.

Government Publications and Reports

JP 5-0: Joint Operations Planning. U.S. Department of Defense Joint Publication (JP). Washington, DC: U.S. Department of Defense, 2011.

FM 3-0: *Operations*. U.S. Dept. of the Army Field Manual (FM). Washington, DC: U.S. Department of the Army, 2008.

FM 3-24: *Counterinsurgency*. U.S. Dept. of the Army Field Manual (FM). Washington, DC: U.S. Department of the Army, 2006.

FM 5-0: Army Planning and Orders Production. U.S. Dept. of the Army Field Manual (FM). Washington, DC: U.S. Department of the Army, 2010.

FM 6-0: *Mission Command: Command and Control of Army Forces*. U.S. Dept. of the Army Field Manual (FM). Washington, DC: U.S. Department of the Army, 2006.

ADP 3-0: *Unified Land Operations*. U.S. Dept. of the Army Doctrine Publication (ADP). Washington, DC: U.S. Department of the Army, 2011.

The TRADOC CBA Guide: *Capabilities-Based Assessment (CBA) Guide Version 3.1*. U.S. Training Doctrine Command (TRADOC), Washington, DC: U.S. Department of the Army Doctrine Publication, 2010.

DOS Guide *US government counterinsurgency guide*. U.S. Department of State Publication, Washington, DC: U.S. Department of State, 2009.

Articles

Bajoria, Jayshree. "North Korea After Kim," Council on Foreign Relations (19 December 2011), http://www.cfr.org/north-korea/north-korea-after-kim/p17322 (accessed 6 April 2012).

Cha, Victor D. "The Rationale For Enhanced Engagement of North Korea: After the Perry Policy Review," Asian Survey (November/December 1999), http://www.jstor.org/discover/10.2307/3021142?uid=3739672&uid=2129&uid=2&uid=70&uid=4&uid=3739256&sid=56006875803 (accessed 6 April 2012).

Clayton, Mattew. "Drugs in the DPRK2006-2011: A Quantitative Analysis," NK News (March 2012), http://nknews.org/wp-content/uploads/2012/03/Comparative-Analysis-on-DPRK-Drugs.pdf (accessed 6 April 2012).

Office of the Korea Chair. "Record of North Korea's Major Conventional Provocations since 1960s," Center for Strategic and International Studies (May 25, 2010), http://csis.org/files/publication/ 100525_ North_Koreas_ Provocations.pdf (accessed 27 September 2011).

Harding, Luke. "After Kim Jong-il's death, what will happen to North Korea's nuclear arsenal?", *the guardian*, http://www.guardian.co.uk/world/2011/dec/19/north-korea-nuclear-arsenal-dangers (accessed 7 January 2012).

Hoffman, Bruce. "Combating Al Qaeda and the Militant Islamic Threat," Testimony presented to the House Armed Services Committee, Subcommittee on Terrorism, Unconventional Threats and Capabilities (February 16, 2006), http://www.rand.org/pubs/testimonies/2006/RAND_CT255.pdf (accessed 3 December 2011).

Kilcullen, David. "Countering Global Insurgency," *Small Wars Journal* (30 November 2004) http://smallwarsjournal. com/documents/kilcullen.pdf (accessed December 3, 2011).

Matheny, Michael R. "The Roots of Modern American Operational Art," http://www.au.af.mil/au/awc/awcgate/army-usawc/modern_operations.pdf (accessed 8 October, 2011).

Nanto, Dick K. "The North Korean Economy: Overview and Policy Analysis," CRS Report for Congress (18 April, 2007) http://www.nautilus.org/publications/essays/napsnet/reports/ 07045CRS.pdf (accessed 27 September).

Nesbitt, Peter. "Joint U.S.-Korea Academic Studies: Emerging Voice," Korea Economic Institute (2011 Special Edition), http://www.keia.org/sites/default/files/publications/ emergingvoices_final_peternesbitt.pdf (accessed 6 April 2012).

Sepp, Kalev I. "Best Practices in Counterinsurgency," Military Review (May-June 2005), http://www.au.af.mil/au/awc/awcgate/milreview/sepp.pdf (accessed 27 July 2011).

Vorontsov, Alexander V. "North Korea's Military-First Policy: A Curse or a Blessing?" Brookings Institution (26 May 2006), http://www.brookings.edu/opinions/2006/ 0526northkorea_vorontsov.aspx (accessed 18 September 2011).

Monograph

Joohoon Kim, "Current Issues Concerning Korea's Anti-Terrorism Programs," Fort Leavenworth, KS: U.S. Army Command and Staff College, Master of Military Art and Science Thesis, 2010.

Websites

Encyclopedia of the Nations, "Korea, North-Infrastructure, power, and communications," http://www.nationsencyclopedia.com/economies/Asia-and-the-Pacific/Korea-North-INFRASTRUCTURE-POWER-AND-COMMUNICATIONS.html (accessed 27 September 2011).

Stars and Stripes, "USFK commander takes war cue from Iraq," (29 June 2007), http://www.stripes.com/news/usfk-commander-takes-war-cue-from-iraq-1.80485 (accessed 19 September 2011).

The Chosun Ilbo," Experts Predict Power Struggle When Kim Jong-il Dies," (12 August 2010), http://english.chosun.com/site/data/html_dir/2010/08/12/2010081200281.html (accessed 19 September 2011).

The Korea Times, "General Thurman urges preparation for North Korea regime collapse," (20 June 2011), http://www.koreatimes.co.kr /www/news/nation/ 2011/06/113_89816.html (accessed 21 July 2011).

The telegraph, "Power struggle rages in North Korean regime," (24 September 2010), http://www.telegraph.co.uk/news/worldnews/asia/northkorea/8022800/Power-struggle-rages-in-North-Korean-regime.html (accessed 19 September 2011).

U.S. Department of State, "Background Note: North Korea," (29 April 2011), http://www.state.gov/r/pa/ei/bgn/2792.htm (accessed 18 September 2011).

U.S. Office of the Director of National Intelligence, "Statement for the Record on the Worldwide Threat Assessment of the U.S. Intelligence Community," (10 February, 2011), http://www.dni.gov/ testimonies/ 20110210_testimony_clapper.pdf (accessed 2 December, 2011).